6/04

Reading American History

Sacagawea, Lewis, and Clark

Written by Melinda Lilly
Illustrated by Belgin Kaya Wedman

Educational Consultants

Kimberly Weiner, Ed.D
Betty Carter, Ed.D

Rourke
Publishing LLC
Vero Beach, Florida 32963

www.rourkepublishing.com

For my husband Mark, who is constant in my life. Thank you for all your support. —B. K. W.

Designer: Elizabeth J. Bender

Library of Congress Cataloging-in-Publication Data

Lilly, Melinda.
   Sacagawea, Lewis, and Clark / Melinda Lilly; illustrated by Belgin Kaya Wedman.
      p. cm. — (Reading American history)
   Summary: A simple description of the nineteenth-century expedition from Missouri to the Pacific Ocean which was undertaken by Meriwether Lewis, William Clark, and the Shoshone Indian Sacagawea.
   ISBN 1-58952-362-8
   1. Lewis and Clark Expedition (1804-1806)—Juvenile literature. 2. Sacagawea 1786-1884—Juvenile literature. Lewis, Meriwether, 1774-1809—Juvenile literature. 4. Clark, William, 1770-1838—Juvenile literature. 5. West (U.S.)—Description and travel—Juvenile literature. [1. Lewis and Clark Expedition (1804-1806) 2. Sacagawea, 1786-1884. 3. Lewis, Meriwether, 1774-1809. 4. Clark, William, 1770-1838.]
   I. Wedman, illus. II. Title.

F592.7 .L73 2002
917.804'2—dc21   2002017045

Cover Illustration: Sacagawea, William Clark, and Meriwether Lewis

Printed in the USA

Time Line

Help students follow this story by introducing important events in the Time Line.

1801   Thomas Jefferson becomes president of the United States.

1803   The Louisiana Purchase more than doubles the size of the U. S.

1804   The Lewis and Clark expedition sets off.

1804   In November, Sacagawea joins the expedition.

1805   Sacagawea gives birth to Jean Baptiste, called "Pomp."

1805   The expedition reaches the Pacific Ocean.

1806   The expedition ends in St. Louis, Missouri.

President Thomas Jefferson had a job for **Meriwether Lewis** and **William Clark**.

They had to find a way to the **Pacific Ocean**.

Looking at the map

Lewis and Clark set off by boat.

They went up the river.

They went into **Native American** lands.

On the way to Native American lands

In 1804, they met **Sacagawea**.

Sacagawea was a Native American.

Sacagawea meets Lewis, Clark, and York.
York was Clark's slave.

Sacagawea helped Lewis and Clark make friends with Native Americans.

Saying hello

Sacagawea gave birth to her son "Pomp" on the trail.

Sacagawea holds "Pomp."
She sits with her husband and Lewis's dog.

13

They raced down fast rivers.
They went a long way from home.

In the boats

Still no ocean!

The **Rocky Mountains** blocked the way.

At the Rocky Mountains

They rode over the Rocky Mountains.

On the mountain trail

At last, they reached the Pacific Ocean.
What a trip it had been!

They reach their goal.

21

Word List

Clark, William (KLARK, WIL yum)—From 1804 to 1806, William Clark explored the West with the expedition called the Corps of Discovery.

Jefferson, Thomas (JEF er sen, TOM us)—The third president of the United States, Thomas Jefferson wrote the Declaration of Independence.

Lewis, Meriwether (LOO is, MARE ee weh thur)— From 1804 to 1806, Meriwether Lewis explored the West with the expedition called the Corps of Discovery.

Native American (NAY tiv uh MER ih kun)—A member of the peoples native to North America; an American Indian

Pacific Ocean (puh SIF ik OH shun)—The biggest ocean in the world

president (PREZ ih dent)—The chief executive of the United States

Rocky Mountains (ROK ee MOUN tunz)—The main mountain range of North America

Sacagawea (sak uh gah WEE uh)—Shoshone woman who explored the West with the expedition called the Corps of Discovery

Books to Read

Adler, David. *A Picture Book of Sacagawea*. Holiday House, 2001.

Bruchac, Joseph. Sacajawea: *The Story of Bird Woman and the Lewis and Clark Expedition*. Silver Whistle, 2000.

Herbert, Janis. *Lewis and Clark for Kids: Their Journey of Discovery with 21 Activities*. Chicago Review, 2000.

Sullivan, George. *Lewis and Clark*. Scholastic, 2000.

Websites to Visit

www.pbs.org/lewisandclark/

www.nationalgeographic.com/lewisclark/

www.lewis-clark.org/

http://lewisandclarktrail.com/

Index